EcoZones

DESERTS

Lynn M. Stone

ROURKE ENTERPRISES, INC.
Vero Beach, FL 32964

Library of Congress Cataloging in Publication Data

Stone, Lynn M.
    Deserts / by Lynn M. Stone.
        p. cm. — (Ecozones)
    Includes index.
    Summary: Examines the desert as an ecological niche and describes the plant and animal life supported there.
    ISBN 0-86592-438-4
    1. Desert ecology — Juvenile literature.   2. Deserts — Juvenile literature. [1. Desert ecology. 2. Ecology.]   I. Title.
II. Series: Stone, Lynn M.   Ecozones.
QH541.5.D4S76   1989
574.5'2652 — dc20   89-32745
                                        CIP
                                        AC

CONTENTS

THE DESERT

It's a familiar scene. A man clutching a canteen staggers across the sand. Behind him stands a spindly, long-armed cactus, its spines frighteningly sharp and long. Overhead, vultures circle in a cloudless sky. The sun beats down unmercifully.

For many people, this scene *is* the American desert, a roofless furnace of sand. Enter the desert, the scene implies, and you will be the main course for vultures as soon as you are properly cooked by the sun.

Actually, the desert is not quite the searing, sandy place it's often shown to be. Make no mistake: the desert can be an extremely harsh, unforgiving environment. It can be frightfully hot, and it can kill. But handled with common sense, the desert can be a delight for anyone who treads upon it. The secret, one which the desert's animals know well, is knowing when to be out and about. Summer days are scorching, but summer nights and the days of spring and fall can be quite pleasant. The desert winter can be uncomfortably cold, or comfortably cool; it depends upon the desert's location.

Opposite Arizona's *Sonoran Desert blooms in spring when annuals like owl clover and lupine blanket the foothills against a backdrop of palo verde trees and saguaro cactus.*

Rather than being just the immense sandbox of the American Southwest, the desert is an active and complex **community** of plants and animals. Certainly some parts of the desert are sandy and barren. Other sections, however, are amazingly rich in plant and animal life. These variations in the abundance and number of species of plants and animals help make the desert a fascinating network of communities with a common thread.

In truth, the desert is really a group of deserts. These deserts often appear to be remarkably different places. Each desert does have its own identity, although many of the characteristics that separate one desert from another are not obvious to untrained eyes. Nevertheless, despite differences in plants, animals, climate, soil, and altitude, the American deserts share a basic theme: dryness.

All of the North American deserts are dry, or **arid**. The key factor in the establishment of a desert is the relatively small amount of water available. Areas that are regularly soaked with rainfall or snow, such as forests, are in no danger of being mistaken for a desert. But how much water—or how little—makes a desert?

Most scientists agree that for an environment to be a true desert, it must receive less than 10 inches of precipitation (rain and snow melt) each year. In addition, a true desert is a site that has a high rate of **evaporation**. When water evaporates, it passes in tiny particles into the air. In the desert, a pool of standing water vanishes into the air rather quickly through the process of evaporation. Therefore, places that have little rainfall but low evaporation are not true deserts. The Arctic region is a typical example. Precipitation in the northern Arctic is very low, but evaporation is also low. The Arctic tends to retain water while deserts lose their surface water.

Curiously enough, the level of heat, cold, or sand in an area does not determine whether or not it is a desert. Instead, it is the amount of dryness, which is related to precipitation (incoming moisture) and evaporation, that determines whether a region is truly a desert.

On an arid landscape, certain plants can survive. These are plants that have evolved over the years in ways that enable them to deal successfully with the desert's dryness. The ways in which plants cope with the desert are called

adaptations. Plants that cannot survive the desert's environmental conditions are excluded from the community. Those plants that can live in the desert form what becomes a more or less typical desert landscape. Where certain desert-adapted plants grow together, then, we can assume that a desert environment exists. Keep in mind, however, that desert plants, even where they prosper, do not grow densely. Indeed, part of the desert's "look" is the scattered appearance of plants.

In North America, the true desert environment exists in a large swath of the West. Desert in one form or another stretches from southern Idaho and southeastern Oregon south into Mexico. That is a huge tract of land, over 2,000 miles from north to south. It includes eight percent of the United States' total land area, about 300,000 square miles. Desert covers almost all of Nevada and significant portions of Oregon, Idaho, Utah, California, Arizona, New Mexico, and Texas. Desert occupies central Mexico from its northern borders with west Texas and New Mexico south several hundred miles. Northwestern Mexico and nearly all of the Baja California peninsula are also desert.

Much of the North American desert

DESERTS

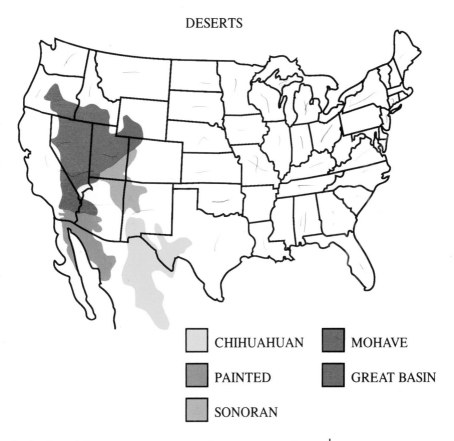

CHIHUAHUAN   MOHAVE

PAINTED   GREAT BASIN

SONORAN

is lodged between mountain ranges, the Sierra Nevada on the west and the Rockies on the east. The peaks flanking the desert reach up to 13,000 feet. The desert itself is considerably lower than that, almost always below 5,000 feet above sea level.

The fact that a large segment of the desert falls between tall mountains does not mean that the desert itself is a flatland. Smaller mountain ranges rise up from the desert. Many of them rise quite abruptly. And while there are fairly level desert plains, there are also regions of hills, canyons, mesas, and rock outcrops.

Another feature of the desert landscape is the playa. Playas are basins that are dry for part of the year or for several years. Many of the dry playas have a characteristic frosting of salt which was left when the lake water receded.

Other features of the desert terrain are **arroyos** and **alluvial fans**. Arroyos are desert streams. Like playas, they are often dry. Alluvial fans are the handiwork of mountain streams and rivers which carry large quantities of soil and gravel, called **alluvium**, to the deserts below. The deposits of dirt and rock spread out in all directions, creating the impression of a gigantic fan.

Elsewhere the deserts are marked by sand dunes, gentle slopes, salt flats, "chimneys" from ancient volcanic action, and natural bridges and arches, the sculptures of water and windblown sand.

Desert climates are typically hot in the summer. Death Valley is consistently a firebox in summer. The average daily high in July is 116°F. These are the days of which desert legends are made.

Winter on the northern desert is cold. Snowfall and sub-zero temperatures are commonplace. Even in the normally warm Sonoran Desert, winter nights occasionally cool to freezing levels. Only in the deserts along the Gulf of California are the nights always frost-free.

Where the environmental conditions that create desert begin to change, the desert changes too. In several places, desert and grassland mix. In others, the desert vanishes into developing forest of evergreen trees or thickets of chaparral shrub.

Like any other environment, the desert is a much more appealing place at certain times than at others. Undoubtedly the most comfortable time to visit the North American deserts is a season other than summer. Spring is perhaps the best time. Skies are clear, the air cool. The desert plants and animals are becoming vigorous again. In the Sonoran Desert of southern Arizona, lizards and snakes emerge from their winter hideouts. Hedgehog and cholla cactus blossom, and meadows of wildflowers—poppies, lupine, marigold, brittlebush—paint the flats and slopes. Can this, visitors often wonder aloud, be desert?

TYPES OF DESERT

The North American desert encompasses a massive land area. Naturally, there are some fundamental differences in the vegetation and landscape within a region so large. **Ecologists**, the scientists who study plant and animal communities, have found several differences in American desert communities. As a matter of fact, while ecologists agree that the desert supports a variety of communities, they don't agree on the number. They don't always agree either on precisely where the deserts begin or where they end. Ecologists do agree that American deserts are of two basic types. One is the northern, or cold, desert. The other is the southern, or hot, desert.

The cold desert is basically a hot desert with longer periods of cold weather. Some parts of desert have virtually no cold weather. The cold desert also has somewhat greater precipitation. Along with differences in climate and precipitation, deserts show variations in soil, altitude, plants, and animals.

The only cold desert in North America is the Great Basin Desert of Nevada, Utah, western Wyoming,

Opposite *Saguaro cactus dominate the Sonoran Desert landscape in much of southern Arizona, but share the hills in spring with patches of annual wildflowers.*

southern Idaho, and southeastern Oregon. Covering nearly 160,000 square miles, the Great Basin is the largest desert wholly within the United States.

The Great Basin Desert doesn't have the variety of plants and animals of warmer deserts. Most of the cactus, yucca, and agave plants we associate with desert terrain do not grow in the Great Basin Desert. Much of this desert is shrubby. Sagebrush and saltbrush are common, and playas are widely scattered throughout the Great Basin.

Despite its lack of variety, the Great Basin is home to several of the "typical" desert animals, such as mule deer, badgers, kangaroo rats, coyotes, burrowing owls, golden eagles, and red-tailed hawks. The desert range of the sage grouse and gray flycatcher is generally limited to the Great Basin. Reptiles, which are abundant on the hot deserts, are relatively scarce in the Great Basin.

Three hot deserts are generally recognized in North America: the Mojave, Sonoran, and Chihuahuan. Some desert ecologists recognize the Painted Desert as a fourth hot desert, but it is more accurately termed a semidesert. Like the Great Basin Desert, the

Mojave falls entirely within the United States. It occupies 54,000 square miles in southern Nevada, southwestern Utah, and southeastern California. Compared to the Great Basin, the Mojave has a greater number of cactus, desert trees, and such desert shrubs as creosote bush. On the whole, it is a lower desert than the Great Basin. Most of its plains lie near 3,000 feet. It is also a warmer desert than the Great Basin, and in many ways it is a transition between the Great Basin and the Sonoran deserts.

The Mojave has 250 species of **annual** flowers. Annuals grow from seeds only rather than from a renewable root system. Over 200 of the Mojave annuals are **endemics**; that is, they grow nowhere else in the world.

In addition to its magnificent wild-flower displays, the Mojave is known for its yucca plants. Yucca stems are sheathed in dagger-like leaves. The many-branched Joshua tree is the most impressive of the yuccas and the Mojave's best-known plant.

The Mojave has a greater variety of animal life than the Great Basin. It contains such desert-loving species as cactus wren, roadrunner, kit fox, desert bighorn sheep, and the Gila monster, a plump, poisonous lizard.

Above *The Mojave Desert's best known attraction is the Joshua Tree, which is really a yucca, shown here in Joshua Tree National Monument, California.*

South of the Mojave, in the southeastern corner of California, across southern Arizona, and in a large area of western Mexico along both sides of the Gulf of California, lies the Sonoran Desert. About two-thirds of the Sonoran's 106,000 square miles is in the Mexican states of Sonora and Baja California.

For most Americans, the Sonoran is *the* desert. It is the land of the giant saguaro cactus and the site of such cities as Tucson, Phoenix, and Yuma. The Sonoran has the most life forms of any North American desert and a variety of "looks."

Part of the Sonoran's richness of life—what scientists call its **biological richness**—stems from its two rainy seasons each year. Rain normally pelts the Sonoran each winter. Accompanied by thunderstorms, it returns in the summer. More short-lived plants are stimulated in an environment with two growing seasons than in an environment with only one. Another factor in the Sonoran's biological wealth is the fact that it is a subtropical desert. Tropical and subtropical environments, those approaching the earth's equator, usually support the growth of more species than locations farther north.

In the Sonoran Desert, <u>cactus</u> are abundant and varied along with desert trees. The Sonoran is sometimes called the "tree desert."

The largest of the cactus include the saguaro, organ pipe, senita, and cardon. Because they are tall and stately, these species sometimes form "cactus forests." Senita and organ pipe barely extend their range into the Sonoran Desert of southern Arizona. Saguaro, of course, are familiar sights in Arizona and Mexico. The cardon is restricted to Mexico.

The Sonoran Desert is also a showplace of smaller cactus—cholla, prickly pear, fishhook, barrel, and hedgehog among them. Nearly all of the cactus produce large, showy blossoms. The pageant of cactus color starts in March and continues through August with each species taking its turn.

Some spectacular views of Sonoran Desert vegetation can be seen in Organ Pipe National Monument, Saguaro National Monument, and in the Tonto National Forest near Phoenix. The Sonoran is not, however, entirely a beautiful desert garden. Some tremendous sand dunes arise from parts of this desert. Elsewhere, the Sonoran landscape has rock outcroppings, rather monotonous valleys of creosote bush and white bur sage, rolling plains, and isolated mountains.

Several types of reptiles live in the Sonoran. Lizards such as the collared, zebra-tailed, and horned are abundant. The Sonoran whipsnake is endemic. Burrowing owls frequent the Sonoran Desert of California. Thrashers, Gambel's quail, roadrunners, doves, hummingbirds, and wrens are numerous throughout much of the Sonoran. Typical desert mammals of the Sonoran include rock squirrels, coyotes, antelope squirrels, and kangaroo rats. The long-nosed bat of Mexico, one of many desert

bats, feeds in the pollen and nectar of agaves and saguaros.

East of the Sonoran Desert lies the Chihuahuan Desert of some 125,000 square miles. Much of it falls in the same latitude as the Sonoran, but it is a desert of generally high elevations. Portions of the Chihuahuan in Mexico are above 6,500 feet, and, partly as a result of its high altitude, the Chihuahuan has several sites with over 100 days per year of freezing temperatures.

The Chihuahuan Desert covers a part of west Texas, part of southern New Mexico, and a large, continuous section of northern and central Mexico.

Above *Monument Valley along the Utah-Arizona border is noted for its magnificent rock formation. This is part of the Painted Desert or Colorado Plateau Semidesert.*

Much of the Mexican states of Chihuahua, Coahuila, Zacatecas, and San Luis Potosi is Chihuahuan Desert. Portions of Durango, Nuevo Leon, and Hidalgo are also Chihuahuan Desert.

The northern Chihuahuan Desert of Texas and New Mexico has none of the tall, columned cactus that grace the Sonoran. The soil conditions, cool winters, and relatively heavy rainfall—eight to twelve inches annually—have prompted the extensive growth of agave, yucca, and grass. In fact, some edges of the Chihuahuan blend with short-grass prairie.

The Chihuahuan Desert has several species of cactus. In Mexico, its tracts of

Below *A mineral, gypsum, has formed these dunes in White Sands National Monument, part of the Chihuahuan Desert.*

tall, columned cactus are reminders of the giant cactus in the Sonoran Desert of Arizona.

Like other North American deserts, the Chihuahuan is a composite of dunes, rocky plains, scattered mountains, and bajadas, a type of slope. Some of the best vistas of the Chihuahuan Desert are in Big Bend National Park, Texas.

The Painted Desert may or may not be a desert. It all depends upon one's definition. Some ecologists lump the Painted Desert with the Great Basin Desert. Others call it the "Colorado Plateau Semidesert." It is clearly a dry, desert-like area. But three-quarters of the region, which includes southeast Utah, southwest Colorado, northern Arizona, and northwest New Mexico, receives over ten inches of precipitation each year.

The Painted Desert's fame lies in its wondrous canyons, rock formations, mesas, and volcanic flows. It is also admired for the changing array of colors that bathe its earth and rocks as the sun shifts location. One of the region's most attractive areas is Petrified Forest National Park. There, visitors walk among **fossilized**, rock-hard tree trunks.

MAKING OF THE DESERT

The petrified forest's fossilized trees make it clear that the desert was not always desert. The Painted Desert, for instance, was once forested with the vegetation of the subtropics. As in the other American deserts, geological forces changed the climate perhaps over five million years ago. Temperatures rose, and rainfall slacked off. The forests disappeared and were succeeded by grassland. As the climate dried and became too arid for grassland, the grasses were replaced by desert vegetation.

The development and continuation of the North American desert is associated with water. The northern desert receives more precipitation than the southern deserts, but no desert receives more than an average of ten inches of precipitation across its whole. Low humidity and high evaporation are also elements in maintaining the desert environment.

Desert rains tend to be sudden and heavy. Much of the water is lost because it runs off the desert's hard, rocky surface. Ten inches of scattered, gentle

Opposite *In Petrified Forest National Park, fossilized tree trunks show that the Painted Desert was once forested with the mighty trees of the subtropics.*

rainfall during a year would produce a greater variety of plants than the desert's hard rains do. However, enough water soaks in so that even a desert has moisture in its soil below six feet. The catch is that the roots of most plants cannot reach the damp soil.

Hard rains not only "run away" from the soil, they erode the desert. The surface flow of water carries sand that buries new plants and washes out the roots of some established plants. Winds also erode the desert, creating unstable soil for plants. All of these environmental conditions help account for the desert's rather scarce plant cover.

All of the North American deserts are basically a series of basins surrounded by mountains. These mountains play a major role in keeping the deserts dry. As cold, rain-filled clouds move from the Pacific Ocean eastward and toward the desert, they are intercepted by the mountains. Passing through the mountains, the clouds are relieved of their moisture. The area immediately east of the mountains lies parched.

PLANTS
OF THE DESERT

Desert vegetation is sparse, but it is diverse and, often enough, quite beautiful. One of the most interesting and remarkable features of desert plants is their ability to grow in a land where water is scarce.

Desert plants have three major problems. One is how to obtain water where little water exists. Another is how to conserve water once it has been obtained. The third is how to avoid being eaten by plant-eating animals. Many plants deal with the animal threat by having spines, bad taste, waxy leaves, or a strong odor. The water problems are more complex.

One means, however, of survival in a dry environment is demonstrated by the scores of spring wildflower species that carpet the hot deserts. Most of these are annuals. They develop, produce seeds, and die. Each generation grows from a new seed rather than the root system of last year's plant. The seeds lie **dormant**, or inactive, during the hot, dry summers. If necessary, they can lie dormant for years. After rain falls, and adequate moisture has been trapped in the

Right *The yellow palo verde tree (center) shares a plot of the Sonoran Desert with yellow blooms of brittlebush and the pink flowers of hedgehog cactus.*

Above *This barrel cactus demonstrates an adaptation of desert plants for water conservation: the elimination of traditional leaves and the enlarged stem used as a reservoir.*

soil, they spring to life and wrap the desert in a momentary sheet of color.

Some plants adapt to the desert environment by remaining small. They require very little water and they remain dormant during the dry months. Several plants have special leaves. Plants lose moisture through their leaves in a process called **transpiration**. It is to the plant's advantage to retain moisture. One type of desert plant has leaf pores that close during the heat of the day. Others reduce water loss by having waxy surfaces.

Most desert plants have lateral roots. Lateral roots spread around the plant in shallow soil. Rain typically does not soak deeply into the soil, and lateral roots can absorb it more easily. The

mesquite and creosote bush, however, use the opposite adaptation. Their roots are deep, so they can always reach ground water.

One of the best-known adaptations of desert plants is the water storage system used by cactus, yuccas, and agaves. These plants, which store water in their leaves and stems, are called **succulents**. By eliminating traditional leaves, cactus have, in effect, eliminated water loss. The enlarged stem of a cactus is actually the plant's reservoir. The normal function of leaves in the plant's food-producing process is taken over by the stem. The cactus obtains its water through a system of shallow, widespread roots.

Above *Each spring, annual wild-flowers—lupine, marigold, owl clover, Mexican gold poppies and others—bloom throughout the desert regions.*

5 ANIMALS OF THE DESERT

Many of the natural barriers that prevent the transport of plants from one desert habitat to another do not affect animals. A coyote can move fairly easily from one desert location to another, or to an altogether different community. For a bird, desert invasion or retreat is even simpler. As a result, many of the animal species of the Sonoran Desert are also found in other deserts. Several desert inhabitants are also found in totally different **biomes**. Badgers, burrowing owls, mule deer, and cougars, for example, live in the desert, but they can live equally well elsewhere. There are other animals, of course, that do not live beyond desert limits. Several kangaroo rat species are an example.

A red-tailed hawk circling a forest of saguaros will catch the observer's eye, but the desert is home to thousands of species of animals that most people never notice. These are the invertebrates, the great collection of bugs, beetles, spiders, centipedes, and their many kin.

The small size of invertebrates tends to hide them. Their generally dull

Opposite *Male sage grouse in spring courtship display on Great Basin Desert.*

coloring and their need to stay out of the heat also contribute to their being overlooked. Like many of the larger desert animals, most of the invertebrates live underground or in ground litter during the day.

Two groups of the desert's well-known invertebrates are scorpions and fuzzy tarantulas. Most species are harmless to man, but the scorpion's stinger and the tarantula's poisonous bite are lethal to their animal prey.

The desert is not a suitable habitat for most amphibians. These soft-skinned animals—the frogs, toads, and salamanders—need adequate moisture to replace lost body fluid.

Land-dwelling reptiles are much better adapted to the desert's terms than amphibians. Their shelled eggs, in contrast to amphibian egg clusters, do not have to be deposited in water. In addition, their covering of scales or shell keeps most of their body moisture inside. Even so, most desert snakes are active at night. Their ideal body temperature, which is regulated by their environment, is usually easier to reach after dark than on sunny days. Lizards, on the other hand, are generally daylight hunters. They can tolerate more heat than the majority of desert snakes.

Twelve varieties of rattlesnakes live in American deserts, and the coral snake lives in the Sonoran. Most desert snakes, including the patchnose, whipsnake, coachwhip, blind snake, ground snake, shovelnose, longnose, and many other species, are non-poisonous.

Permanent desert ponds and rivers have a few aquatic turtle species. The desert proper has desert tortoises in the Mojave and Sonoran, and ornate box turtles range into the Chihuahuan. Both of these land turtles rely on a diet of succulent plants for much of their liquid intake. Their shells offer protection against predators and nearly eliminate water loss.

Above *The regal horned lizard blends in perfectly with the desert ground around it.*

33

Right *The Gila woodpecker is restricted to the Sonoran Desert.*

Right *The cactus wren, shown here at its nest in a cholla cactus, is found throughout the hot deserts.*

Desert bird life is somewhat limited by the types of vegetation, the summer heat, and the scarcity of permanent water. Still, the desert region has a fair number of birds of prey—the golden eagle, hawks, owls, and vultures—and a variety of quail, thrashers, doves, wrens, woodpeckers, flycatchers, and several other species.

The Gila woodpecker and the elf owl are particularly well-adapted for the desert. The woodpecker drills saguaro cactus for insect larvae. The woodpecker also hammers out nest holes in the saguaro. The holes cause no lasting damage because the saguaro oozes a healing sap over the cavity walls. When the woodpecker abandons its cactus berth, it is apt to be taken over by an elf owl.

Other characteristic desert birds are the roadrunner, black-throated sparrow, and cactus wren. The cactus wren is the largest of the wrens. It often builds a gourd-shaped nest in the prickly branches of cholla cactus. Miraculously, the wren also seems to avoid spearing itself on a cactus joint.

Desert mammals are an assorted lot, ranging in size from mice and rats to mountain lions, bighorn sheep, and pronghorns. The large desert mammals are difficult to see. Their coloration blends with the desert, and many of them, such as the bighorns, live in extremely rugged country. Most desert hikers are far more likely to see bats or rodents than large mammals. Another problem with observing desert mammals is that most of them are **nocturnal**; they are active at night but not during the day.

Mammals have found several ways to adapt to desert conditions, particu-

Right *The desert bighorn, one of the desert herbivores, has become scarce after contact with the diseases of domestic sheep.*

Right *The desert bobcat is one of the largest desert predators.*

larly the low availability of water and the seasonal heat. One of the most obvious adaptations is the ability to burrow underground. When air temperatures reach 105°F, the soil surface reaches up to 170°F. But just 18 inches underground, the temperature holds in the 80's. A burrow also protects its residents against sand and dust storms.

A unique adaptation to the desert is demonstrated by the Merriam's kangaroo rat. It has specialized kidneys to process its liquid wastes. The kangaroo rat flushes its system without using much water; its wastes are extremely concentrated instead of being diluted by water. Another adaptation shared by several rodents and birds is the ability to survive on plentiful dry seeds. These animals actually take water from the seeds as well as solid nourishment.

Above *Merriam's kangaroo rat is one of several species found in the North American deserts.*

THE FLOW OF ENERGY

The desert's plants and animals share a similar environment; they live together in a community. As in a human community, the natural community of desert plants and animals has "jobs" to be filled in order for the community to function. Each plant and animal fills one, or more, of these jobs, or **niches**. Since each animal has its own special niche, it is able to obtain food without serious competition from other species. The red-tailed hawk, for example, is a **predator**, or hunter. That is its role in the community. But the great-horned owl is also a flying predator. How do they avoid each other? The red-tailed hawk wheels over the desert by day as it looks for rodents or other prey. The great-horned owl, looking for similar prey, flies at night when the hawk has retired to its roost.

When the community functions in an orderly manner, energy travels throughout the community. Each plant and animal functions because it has the energy to do so. The energy that plant and animals use comes from food.

Opposite As the Harris' antelope squirrel munches on plant material, the sun's energy moves another link on the chain.

Desert plants manufacture, or produce, food. Plants, then, are **producers**. Plants convert the sun's energy into simple plant sugar in a process called **photosynthesis**. The sugar is used by the plant, in association with water and nutrients from the air, to grow and reproduce.

When an insect bores into an organ pipe cactus, it is taking some of the food—and energy—stored in the cactus. In this way, some of the sun's energy, once stored in the tissues of the cactus, has been unlocked and passed to the insect. The insect may be eaten by a woodpecker. Once again the energy has moved. The insect and the woodpecker are both **consumers**; they consume, rather than manufacture, food.

In the desert community, all of the animals are consumers. Some of them, however, consume only, or mostly, plants. These are the **herbivores**, the plant-eaters. Other animals consume animals. These are **carnivores**, the meat-eaters. A few animals, such as the box turtle, eat plant and animal material. Such animals are called **omnivores**. When each of these groups of animals is allowed to live without interference, each group helps to maintain, or balance, the other.

Within the desert there are countless links between animals and between the animals and plants. These links serve the purpose of exchanging energy. As one animal uses another animal or a plant for food, energy moves another step in a chain of sorts. Ultimately, every animal falls prey to something else. Even the largest, fiercest animals become prey for man or for the tiny germs that cause disease.

When animals die, their bodies are ultimately destroyed by *decomposers.* These are plants and animals that, by eating the dead animal, begin the process of returning that animal to the air and soil. As decomposers process the animal, they eventually reduce it to particles that become part of the air and soil. In having been decomposed, or eaten, by a variety of organisms, large and small, the dead animal is being turned into forms usable for plant food. The energy that began in the plant tissues thus flows through the community and finally back to plants.

7 CONSERVATION OF THE DESERT

Many people who do not live on the desert or who have never seen the living desert do not hold it in high regard. Much of the desert has been left alone largely because of its great size and its harshness, not because people have necessarily wanted to protect it. Like other natural communities, however, the desert has suffered from the impact of civilization.

The early inhabitants of the American desert were Indians. The Pima, Papago, Hopi, Navajo, and others learned to live off the desert's meager resources. They made clothing from the fibers of desert plants. They gathered fruit from prickly pear cactus and other edibles. They cultivated small farms and made little homes from the desert's natural resources. They developed amazingly hardy strains of beans and corn. The Indians' impact on the desert's native plants and animals was minimal.

Today man is finding more and more uses for the desert. Cities like Yuma, Phoenix, Las Vegas, and Tucson have become major population centers in the desert. As desert cities expand,

Opposite *Sonoran Desert in spring at Organ Pipe Cactus National Monument.*

they sprawl deeper into the desert. As more people discover the dry, healthful climate of the desert, desert cities continue to grow.

Another impact on the desert has been the conversion of desert vegetation to cropland. Crops are being nourished by water pumped from underground. Unfortunately, desert cities are pumping more water from the underground storage basins than nature is returning through precipitation.

Elsewhere, the desert is being tapped for gold, silver, copper, mercury, and other minerals. It is being used for military activities, as a burial ground for atomic wastes, and for the construction of sunny resorts. Here and there, desert vegetation has been disfigured by cactus collectors and off-road vehicles.

The desert has lost most of its bighorn sheep to the diseases brought by domestic sheep. Mexico's Sonoran grizzly bears are gone, and the desert wolves of Mexico, the *lobos,* are nearly gone. The desert tortoise has been hounded toward oblivion by collectors.

But much of the great American desert remains as it was, unspoiled and unpopulated. Several outstanding sections have been protected in national parks, national monuments, and other public lands. Great Basin National Park, one of the newest in the national park system, protects a portion of the desert that bears its name. Environmentalists are actively trying to create additional desert parks in Arizona and California. With reasonable care, much of the North American desert will remain unspoiled for generations to come.

GLOSSARY

adaptation a characteristic of function, form, or behavior that improves an organism's survival chances in a particular habitat

alluvium clay, silt, sand, gravel, or other material deposited by running water

alluvial fan the deposits of alluvium that spread into a fan shape

annual a plant which blooms from seed and lasts only one season

arid dry

arroyo a desert stream or gully

biological relating to a living thing

biome a large, natural community characterized by the plants that dominate the community, such as a desert or forest

carnivore meat-eating animal

community all the plants and animals linked by food chains in a particular habitat

consumer an animal, so named because it must eat, or consume, to live

decomposer an organism, most often bacterium and fungi, that consumes dead tissue and reduces it to small particles

dormant a state of inactivity due to the slowing or stopping of normal functions

ecologist a scientist who studies the interrelationships of plants and animals in association with their environment

endemic an organism restricted in its range to a particular, small location

evaporate the disappearance of water in minute particles into the air

fossilized to have been changed into a preserved, hard form

herbivore plant-eating animal

niche an organism's role or job in the community

nocturnal active at night

omnivore an animal with the capability to eat both plant and animal material

photosynthesis the process by which green plants produce simple food sugars through the use of sunlight and chlorophyll

predator an animal that kills and feeds on other animals

producer a green plant, so named for its ability to manufacture, or produce, food

succulent a fleshy plant that stores liquid in its stem or leaves

transpiration the process by which water evaporates from plant tissues

46

DESERT SITES

The following is a sampling of outstanding sites where you can expect to find characteristic plants and animals of the desert and outstanding desert scenery:

UNITED STATES

Arizona

Cabeza Prieta National Wildlife Range, Yuma, Arizona
Organ Pipe Cactus National Monument, Ajo, Arizona
Petrified Forest National Park, Holbrook, Arizona
Saguaro National Monument, Tucson, Arizona
Tonto National Forest, Phoenix, Arizona

California

Anza-Borrego Desert State Park, Borrego Springs, California
Death Valley National Monument, Death Valley, California
Joshua Tree National Monument, Twentynine Palms, California
Providence Mountains State Recreation Area, Essex, California

Nevada

Desert National Wildlife Range, Las Vegas, Nevada
Great Basin National Park, Baker, Nevada
Ruby Lake National Wildlife Refuge, Elko, Nevada

New Mexico

Bosque del Apache National Wildlife Refuge, San Antonio, New Mexico
Carlsbad Caverns National Park, Carlsbad, New Mexico
White Sands National Monument, Alamogordo, New Mexico

Texas

Big Bend National Park, Texas

Utah

Arches National Park, Moab, Utah
Capitol Reef National Park, Torrey, Utah
Zion National Park, Springdale, Utah

ACTIVITIES

Here are some activities and projects that will help you learn more about the North American deserts:

1. Choose a desert animal and tell how it is specially made (adapted) for life in the desert environment.

2. Draw a map of North America and show the extent of desert. Illustrate your map with drawings or pictures of typical desert plants and animals such as saguaro cactus, kangaroo rats, roadrunners, and lizards.

3. Draw a desert food chain or several desert food chains, showing the relationship of sunlight to plants, plants to animals, and animals to each other.

4. Report on one of the major desert reserves in the United States. (See the list in this book for ideas.) Write to the appropriate site for information.

5. Create a collage of desert scenes, plants, and animals.

INDEX

Numbers in boldface type refer to photo pages.